NATURE UNLEASHED

EARTHQUAKES

Louise and Richard Spilsbury

W
FRANKLIN WATTS
LONDON·SYDNEY

Franklin Watts
First published in Great Britain in 2016 by The Watts Publishing Group

Credits
Series Editors: Sarah Eason and Harriet McGregor
Series Designer: Simon Borrough
Picture Researcher: Rachel Blount

Picture credits: Cover: Shutterstock: Petrafler (top), Somjin Klong-ugkara (bottom); Inside: NOAA: NGDC, M. Mehrain, Dames and Moore 13t 13b; Shutterstock: Tracy Ben 19, Marisa Estivill 6–7, Everett Historical 21, Fotos593 4–5, IgorGolovniov 23, Junrong 25t, 25b, Shawn Kashou 17, Somjin Klong-ugkara 1, 11; Wikimedia Commons: UN Photo/Logan Abassi United Nations Development Programme 27, Arnold Genthe, Library of Congress 9, NOAA 7r, Uwebart 14–15.

Every attempt has been made to clear copyright. Should there be any inadvertent omission please apply to the publisher for rectification.

HB ISBN: 978 1 4451 5391 9

Printed in China

Franklin Watts
An imprint of
Hachette Children's Group
Part of The Watts Publishing Group
Carmelite House
50 Victoria Embankment
London EC4Y 0DZ

An Hachette UK Company
www.hachette.co.uk

www.franklinwatts.co.uk

Contents

EARTHQUAKE DANGER

Earthquakes are natural events that can cause deadly disasters. In an earthquake, the Earth's surface moves and trembles. The solid ground beneath buildings, roads and homes shakes and can break open huge cracks in the land.

This road in Ecuador cracked open on 18 April 2016 after a 7.8 **magnitude** earthquake.

How Dangerous?

Some earthquakes are small. People may hardly notice that they happen or they may simply see a lamp swinging slightly on the ceiling or a glass gently shaking on a table. Other earthquakes are huge. As the ground moves, whole buildings can **collapse** and the air fills with a sound like an aeroplane roaring past. Earthquakes can cause more damage than any other type of natural disaster.

Measuring Disaster

When an earthquake happens the ground shakes and moves.

Seismologists use **seismometers** to measure how much the ground shakes.

Small changes in the Earth's **crust** – such as vibrations – can occur before an earthquake.

Seismologists study images taken by **satellites** to measure the shape of and changes to the Earth's crust.

Scientists have devised the **Richter scale** to compare different earthquakes. On the scale, 1 is the smallest and 10 is the greatest. A 5.3 is a moderate earthquake.

The Richter scale measures an earthquake by its strength, or magnitude. A magnitude 5.3 is a moderate earthquake. A 6.3 is a strong earthquake.

Natural disasters have taken place since the Earth was formed. People have many ways of deciding what the world's worst natural disasters have been, from the deadliest disaster to the costliest. This book includes some of the worst earthquakes in history.

EARTHQUAKES IN ACTION

How do earthquakes happen? The Earth moves and shakes during a quake because of movements deep below its surface.

Plates on the Move

The Earth's crust is a layer of rock, which covers the surface of the planet. It consists of huge, rocky slabs that fit together like a jigsaw puzzle. These are called **tectonic plates**. The plates float like enormous rafts on hot, soft and liquid rock called **magma** that lies deep inside the Earth. The edges of the plates are called plate boundaries. The plates are constantly and very slowly moving around, sliding past and bumping into each other.

A rift valley is a long, deep crack in the Earth's surface formed where the tectonic plates have moved apart.

Faults

An earthquake happens when two of the Earth's plates suddenly slip past one another. The weak area where two plates meet is called a **fault**. The edges of the plates are jagged and rough. As they push against each other, pressure builds up until suddenly the two edges come apart and move past each other, causing an earthquake. The location directly above where the earthquake starts is called the **epicentre**. When the plates shift, they make the land all around them move too.

A Powerful Quake

One of the most powerful earthquakes ever happened in Alaska in 1964. It measured 9.2 on the Richter scale and was felt over a wide area. It caused lots of damage and 131 people were killed. The reason so few lives were lost is that the quake happened in a place where not many people lived.

The 1964 Alaskan earthquake lasted 3 minutes, causing **landslides** and **tsunamis** that resulted in widespread damage.

10 SAN FRANCISCO

The earthquake that struck San Francisco, California, in the United States, at 5.12 a.m. on the morning of 18 April 1906 was one of the worst natural disasters in the history of the country. It was also one of the worst earthquakes of all time.

- Coos Bay
- San Francisco
- Los Angeles

UNITED STATES

The San Andreas Fault

The San Andreas Fault

San Francisco lies on the San Andreas Fault. There had been quakes along this fault before, but this one cracked the ground along the fault line for about 480 kilometres (km). That is almost half the length of California. The earthquake shook the ground for a full minute. It toppled buildings and damaged fuel and power lines, which set off devastating fires.

On the Record

Experts believe that the 1906 earthquake must have measured 7.8 on the Richter scale. It killed between 700 and 3,000 people.

The earthquake was one of the strongest ever felt in North America. The shock reached all the way to Coos Bay, Oregon, to Los Angeles, California, and as far east as central Nevada, an area of about 970,000 **square kilometres** (sq km).

The 1906 San Francisco earthquake was the world's first major natural disaster to be recorded in photographs.

Fires burned out of control for three days and nights. Some of the fires reached temperatures of 1,480 degrees Celsius (°C). The fires destroyed one-quarter of the city.

The earthquake destroyed 28,000 buildings and left more than 225,000 of the city's 400,000 residents homeless.

9 NEPAL

On 25 April 2015 a massive earthquake rocked Nepal between the capital city Kathmandu and the city of Pokhara, 200 km away. The disaster killed almost 9,000 people and injured thousands more. It also flattened or damaged over 850,000 homes, as well as schools, clinics and other buildings.

Nepal

Pokhara • • • Mount Everest
Kathmandu

Aftershocks

The earthquake measured 7.8 on the Richter scale. It was followed by dangerous **aftershocks**. Aftershocks are smaller earthquakes that happen a short time after a big earthquake in the same area. As well as a large number of smaller aftershocks, there was also a very damaging one that measured 7.3, on 12 May 2015. Even more than a year later, many of the buildings in damaged areas remained piles of rubble. Many people continue to live in tents and other temporary homes.

On the Record

One of the worst-hit areas was Sindhupalchok. More than 2,000 people died in this district alone. In Kathmandu, over 1,000 people lost their lives.

Thousands of people were killed or badly injured when they were hit by collapsing buildings or by falling **debris**. Mount Everest was also struck by deadly **avalanches** caused by the quake.

The earthquake destroyed many buildings in Kavreplanchok district, Nepal.

After the earthquakes, many people slept in tents and shelters around Kathmandu for weeks. Some people had lost their homes, but others were too afraid to sleep in buildings in case there were more aftershocks.

This was the worst earthquake to hit Nepal for 80 years. The disaster affected more than eight million people, many living in **remote** and mountainous areas of the country.

8 IRAN

Night-time earthquakes can be especially dangerous because people are not able to get to safety. On 21 June 1990 at 12.30 a.m. a magnitude 7.7 earthquake shook the shores of the Caspian Sea in northern Iran. People were sleeping in their simply built homes, which could not withstand the quake and the aftershocks that followed.

Rudbar • Manjil
Lushan

Iran

Shaking Soils

The earthquake's epicentre was very close to the surface so it was very destructive. The land in this area consists of large amounts of sand and mud, which shakes a lot more than hard rock, causing much more damage. The earthquake also caused **liquefaction**. This is when the damp ground can no longer support the weight of buildings above. The buildings fall into the crumbling land beneath them.

On the Record

An area of 50,000 sq km was absolutely devastated.

The earthquake destroyed the cities of Rudbar, Manjil, Lushan and 700 villages. At least 300 other villages were also damaged.

The earthquake killed about 40,000 people and injured 60,000 more.

In this mountain village near Manjil, most buildings were made of dried mud and collapsed instantly during the quake.

During the dark night hours that followed the quake, it was difficult for help to reach remote mountain villages. Landslides and rubble blocked paths and roads, preventing ambulances and rescue vehicles from getting through.

This elevated concrete water tank collapsed. The tank was 46 m high and was two-thirds full at the time of the earthquake.

Approximately 100,000 buildings collapsed or were damaged, leaving 500,000 people without homes.

13

7 PERU

At 3.20 p.m. on 31 May 1970 the deadliest earthquake South America has ever known shook Peru. The quake had a magnitude of 7.9. The epicentre was under the Pacific Ocean about 25 km west of the coastal town of Chimbote, in north-central Peru.

Mount Huascarán
Chimbote
Lima

Peru

Coastal Catastrophe

The most damage occurred in the coastal towns near the epicentre, but the effects of the quake were felt in Peru's capital city, Lima, more than 650 km away. People were also killed by a series of landslides when the earthquake dislodged rock and ice at the tops of mountains. About 70,000 people were killed in the disaster and more than 800,000 were made homeless.

On the Record

The earthquake lasted 45 seconds and damaged or destroyed roads, bridges and buildings over an area of 83,000 sq km. This is an area bigger than Belgium and the Netherlands together!

Many of the homes and buildings in the area were made from **adobe**, a type of clay mud, and they were built on loose soil. Most people were killed or injured when their homes or businesses collapsed.

This picture shows the area that was covered by the landslide from Mount Huascarán.

The worst landslide occurred on Mount Huascarán. A mass of snow, water and mud sped down its side at up to 200 kilometres per hour (kph), destroying nearby towns.

The city of Yungay was filled with mud up to 30 metres (m) deep by landslides.

6 KASHMIR, PAKISTAN

The earthquake that struck the western Himalayan mountain region at 8.50 a.m. on 8 October 2005 had devastating effects. Its epicentre was just 19 km north-east of Muzaffarabad city and district in Kashmir, and 105 km away from Islamabad, the capital of Pakistan.

AFGHANISTAN

Islamabad • • Muzaffarabad
• Delhi

INDIA

Kashmir, Pakistan

Far-Reaching Tremors

The earthquake's magnitude was 7.6 and the Muzaffarabad district was worst hit. The quake also caused major damage in northern Pakistan, northern India and Afghanistan. The **tremors** were felt 1,000 km away in Delhi, the capital city of India.

On the Record

The earthquake actually made a crack in the planet's surface that **geologists** call a **surface rupture**. In some places, the earthquake shifted the ground more than 5 m.

The total number of people killed by the earthquake, its aftershocks and the landslides it caused was around 86,000. More than 69,000 people were injured.

The earthquake made four million people homeless, forcing them to live in tents.

The quake destroyed entire villages, and over 32,000 homes collapsed in cities in Kashmir. Buildings were also destroyed and damaged in Pakistan.

Rescuers could not get through to many of the victims of the disaster because of aftershocks.

5 SICHUAN, CHINA

On 12 May 2008 as people were going about their everyday lives in Sichuan, China, a fault beneath the Earth's surface ruptured. Nothing could have prepared them for over two minutes of violent shaking. The epicentre was just 80 km from the vast city of Chengdu, and was 19 km below the surface.

● Chengdu   ● Shanghai

Sichuan, China

Awful Impacts

The 7.9 magnitude earthquake was the strongest to strike China since 1950. Tremors were felt as far away as Shanghai, 1,700 km from the epicentre. The effects of the disaster were terrible, not just because of the strength of the quake but because the area was so densely **populated**. Many of the buildings were made from mud bricks and were unable to cope with the shaking.

On the Record

More than 87,150 people were killed or declared missing. Over 5,000 children died when the schools they were in collapsed.

Most people died immediately after the earthquake tremors, but hundreds more died later because rescuers could not reach them in their remote mountain homes and villages.

The earthquake destroyed 80 per cent of all the buildings in the area.

Falling debris and collapsing buildings injured a staggering 375,000 people.

More than 1.5 million homes were destroyed and 4.8 milion people were left homeless by the disaster.

4 KANTŌ, JAPAN

On 1 September 1923, as hundreds of people stood beside Yokohama's docks waving off a luxury steamship, the worst earthquake to strike Japan in the twentieth century hit. The huge 7.9 magnitude earthquake spilled people and cars into the sea and crumbled buildings in Tokyo and Yokohama, devastating the whole Kantō region.

Tokyo

Kamakura Yokohama

Kantō, Japan

Lunchtime Fires

The disaster was made worse by the fact that it hit at lunchtime when workers, students and families were sitting down to a cooked meal. Shaking from the quake caused considerable damage but the tremors also knocked over stoves, which started fires. The flames were whipped up by strong winds and spread rapidly through the cities.

On the Record

In Yokohama, nine out of ten homes were destroyed or damaged. In Tokyo, 350,000 homes were wiped out, leaving more than half of the city's inhabitants with no place to live.

It is thought that up to 140,000 people died in this disaster.

The fires caused by the Great Kantō earthquake swept through Yokohama and Tokyo, burning everything and everyone in their path.

The earthquake lasted 4–10 minutes and set off a tsunami that reached 12 m high. The giant waves carried thousands of people into the sea and to their deaths.

The Great Kantō earthquake was so powerful that it not only damaged the base of a 84-tonne bronze statue of Great Buddha at Kamakura, but people say it also made the statue move forwards by about 60 centimetres (cm).

3 MESSINA, ITALY

On 28 December 1908 at approximately 5.20 a.m., the most destructive earthquake ever to hit Europe shook southern Italy. The cities of Messina and Reggio Calabria were worst hit, but the effects of the earthquake and the fires and tsunami that followed were felt in most of southern Italy's coastal towns.

ITALY

Messina   Reggio Calabria
Sicily

Messina, Italy

A Double Disaster

The 7.5 magnitude earthquake lasted for about 20 seconds. Its epicentre was in the Messina Strait, the narrow passage of water that separates the island of Sicily from Calabria on mainland Italy. Moments after the quake, a tsunami formed, crashing into dozens of cities along both coastlines. More than 80,000 people were killed in this double disaster.

On the Record

The violent shaking destroyed or damaged almost all of the buildings in Messina and Reggio Calabria. It broke fuel pipes and caused widespread fires.

The tsunami that followed brought waves that were estimated to be 12 m high flooding onto the shores of northern Sicily and southern Calabria.

Many of southern Italy's cities were devastated by the earthquake.

Some experts believe that the tsunami may not have been caused directly by the quake but by an underwater landslide, which happened seconds after the shock.

In the days after the main earthquake, there were hundreds of smaller aftershocks. These brought down many of the remaining buildings and injured or killed those trying to help victims of the first quake.

2 TANGSHAN, CHINA

On 28 July 1976, in Tangshan, China an earthquake hit that was so strong it was reported to have thrown people up into the air. It was one of the deadliest quakes of the twentieth century, killing more than 242,000 people.

Beijing

Tangshan, China

Massive Tremors

The epicentre of the main 7.5 magnitude earthquake was in the southern part of the industrial city of Tangshan, 110 km east of the capital, Beijing. There was also a huge 7.5 magnitude aftershock later the same day, 70 km away. As well as the high death toll, more than 700,000 people were injured.

On the Record

This sculpture of the residents of Tangshan in 1976 commemorates the disaster.

The main quake lasted about 16 seconds. It made the deep sandy soil in the region behave like a liquid, so most of the buildings in the affected area collapsed.

The earthquake bent and buckled railway lines and collapsed road bridges.

More than 85 per cent of the buildings in Tangshan were destroyed or badly damaged, and some buildings were damaged in cities as far away as Beijing.

The main earthquake struck at 3.42 a.m., when most people were at home in bed. Most of those killed died when the tremors made their **unreinforced** stonework homes collapse on top of them.

The large aftershock caused more deaths and damage and made it even harder for rescuers to help victims trapped under collapsed buildings.

1 HAITI

The epicentre of the earthquake that hit Haiti at 4.53 p.m. on 12 January 2010 was just 25 km south-west of the capital city Port au Prince. This enormous disaster affected around three million people, one-third of the country's population, making it the worst disaster in recent history.

CUBA

Port au Prince

JAMAICA

PUERTO RICO

DOMINICAN REPUBLIC

Haiti

Shaking at the Surface

Haiti's worst quake in two centuries was a magnitude 7.0 event and it happened just 13 km below the surface. The fact that the quake was shallow made the movement of the land above it even worse. People felt the ground below their feet shake all across Haiti and the Dominican Republic, and in Cuba, Jamaica and Puerto Rico. In the years that followed the quake Haiti was slowly rebuilt. Roads were cleared and government buildings reconstructed. However 200,000 people lived in tent camps and badly damaged homes for years.

On the Record

The main quake was shortly followed by two aftershocks of magnitudes 5.9 and 5.5. Over the following days, there were more aftershocks, including one of magnitude 5.9 on 20 January.

The highest number of deaths occurred in the capital, where 2.8 million people lived, many in narrow streets and in buildings not equipped to cope with a quake.

About 220,000 people were killed by the earthquake and aftershocks, and more than 300,000 people were injured.

About one million people were left homeless by the catastrophe.

The earthquake destroyed 100,000 houses and badly damaged almost 200,000 more.

The quake left 19 million **cubic metres** (cu m) of rubble and debris in Port au Prince.

WHERE IN THE WORLD?

This map shows the locations of the earthquakes featured in this book.

Messina, Italy

Iran

Tangshan, China

Sichuan, China

Nepal

Kashmir, Pakistan

INDIAN OCEAN

Why do you think it is important to study earthquakes that have happened in the past? How could this help to save lives and buildings today?

Read the case studies about Haiti, the number one earthquake in this book, and San Francisco, the number ten earthquake. How do they differ?

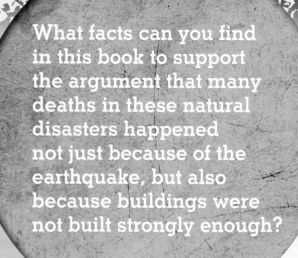

What facts can you find in this book to support the argument that many deaths in these natural disasters happened not just because of the earthquake, but also because buildings were not built strongly enough?

San Francisco

Kantō, Japan

PACIFIC OCEAN

ATLANTIC OCEAN

Haiti

How does the time of day of an earthquake affect the number of deaths or injuries? How do earthquakes cause terrible fires?

Peru

GLOSSARY

adobe a type of clay used as a building material

aftershocks smaller earthquakes that happen shortly after a big earthquake

avalanches masses of snow, ice or rocks that slide rapidly down mountainsides

collapse when something suddenly falls or gives way

crust the Earth's outer layer of solid rock

cubic metres volume; 1 cu m is a cube that is 1 metre on each side

debris loose waste material

epicentre point on the Earth's surface above the place where an earthquake started

fault the place where two or more different tectonic plates meet

geologists scientists who study the Earth and how it is made

landslides the collapses of masses of earth or rock from a mountain or cliff

liquefaction when the strength or stiffness of soil is reduced by the movement of the ground

magma hot, liquid rock below the Earth's surface

magnitude size, particularly of an earthquake

populated inhabited or full of people; people that live in an area populate it

remote far from main centres of population

Richter scale scale that tells people how powerful an earthquake is

satellites objects in space that travel around the Earth

seismologists scientists who study earthquakes

seismometers machines that measure the movement of the ground during a volcanic eruption or earthquake

square kilometres area; 1 sq km is a square that has sides 1 km long

surface rupture when movement on a fault deep within the Earth breaks through to the surface

tectonic plates the giant pieces of rock that fit together like a jigsaw puzzle to form the Earth's crust

tremors the shaking of the ground

tsunamis huge waves caused by an underwater earthquake or landslide

unreinforced something that does not have a strong construction

FURTHER READING

Books

Earthquakes and Volcanoes (Fascinating Facts), Collins

Earth-Shattering Earthquakes (Horrible Geography),
Anita Ganeri, Scholastic

Volcano and Earthquake (Eyewitness), DK Children

Websites

Watch some fascinating clips of earthquakes at:
www.bbc.co.uk/science/earth/natural_disasters/earthquake

Click the links on this interactive image to find out all about
earthquakes at:
www.dkfindout.com/uk/earth/earthquakes

Click through the pages to find out how earthquake-proof
builings are constructed at:
**science.howstuffworks.com/engineering/structural/earthquake-
resistant-buildings.htm**

Note to parents and teachers
Every effort has been made by the Publisher to ensure that
these websites contain no inappropriate or offensive material.
However, because of the nature of the Internet, it is impossible
to guarantee that the contents of these sites will not be altered.
We strongly advise that Internet access is supervised by a
responsible adult.

INDEX

These are the lists of contents for each title in *Nature Unleashed*:

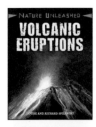

Volcanic Eruptions

Volcano Danger • Volcanoes in Action • Mount St. Helens • Pinatubo • El Chichón • Mount Vesuvius • Santa Maria • Nevado del Ruiz • Mount Pelee • Krakatau • Santorini • Mount Tambora • Where in the World? • Glossary • For More Information • Index

Earthquakes

Earthquake Danger • Earthquakes in Action • San Francisco, 1906 • Nepal, 2015 • Manjil-Rudbar, Iran, 1990 • Peru, 1970 • Kashmir, 2005 • Sichuan, 2008 • Japan, 1923 • Messina, Italy, 1908 • Tangshan, 1976 • Haiti ,2010 • Where in the World? • Glossary • For More Information • Index

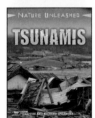

Tsunamis

Tsunami Danger • Tsunamis in Action • Flores Sea, Indonesia, 1992 • Chile, 1960 • Nankaido, Japan, 1946 • Tokaido, Japan 1923 • Papua New Guinea • San-Riku, Japan, 1933 • Andaman Sea-East Coast, 1941 • Moro Gulf, Philippines, 1976 • Japan, 2011 • Indian Ocean, 2004 • Where in the World? • Glossary • For More Information • Index

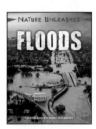

Floods

Flood Danger • Floods in Action • Mississippi Floods • Pakistan Floods, 2010 • Johnstown, 1889 • North Sea Floods, 1953 • North India Floods, 2013 • Vargas Tragedy, Venezuela, 1999 • Bangladesh, 1974 • Yangtse River Flood, 1998 • Ganges Delta, 1970 • Yellow River, China, 1931 • Where in the World? • Glossary • For More Information • Index

Hurricanes

Wind and Storm Danger • Tropical Storms in Action • Great Galveston Hurricane, 1900 • Typhoon Nina, 1975 • Hurricane Katrina, 2005 • Typhoon Bopha, 2012 • Hurricane Mitch, 1998 • Typhoon Tip, 1979 • Hurricane Camille, 1969 • Labor Day Hurricane, 1935 • Hurricane Patricia, 2015 • Typhoon Haiyan, 2013 • Where in the World? • Glossary • For More Information • Index

Wildfires

Fire Danger • Fires in Action • 2010 Russia • Ash Wednesday, 1983 • Landes Forest, 1949 • Black Saturday, 2009 • Miramichi, 1825 • Black Dragon, 1987 • Matheson Fire, 1916 • Cloquet Fire, 1918 • Peshtigo Fire, 1871 • Indonesia, 2015 • Where in the World? • Glossary • For More Information • Index